WHAT WE LOVE

BY
ED MEEK

BLUE LIGHT PRESS ◆ 1ST WORLD LIBRARY

1st WORLD
LIBRARY
Literary Society

AUSTIN ◆ FAIRFIELD ◆ DELHI

Winner of the 2006 Blue Light Book Award

WHAT WE LOVE

1ST WORLD LIBRARY
PO Box 2211, Fairfield, Iowa 52556
www.1stworldlibrary.com

BLUE LIGHT PRESS
PO Box 642, Fairfield, Iowa 52556

COVER AND BOOK DESIGN:
By Melanie Gendron

COVER PHOTO:
By Eddie Meek

AUTHOR PHOTO:
By Elizabeth Meek

FIRST EDITION

LIBRARY OF CONGRESS CONTROL NUMBER:
2006938844

ISBN: 978-1-59540-899-0

ACKNOWLEDGMENTS

Some of these poems have appeared in *The Oregon Review, Cream City Review, Yankee, Troubadour, College English, The Christian Science Monitor, Poem, The Ohio Poetry Review, Classical Antiquity, Classical Outlook, The Larcom Review, 96 Inc., The Worcester Review, Light, The Aurorian, Petroglyph, The Carriage House Review, Green Fuse, Aethlon, Pudding Magazine, Stickman Review.*

This book is dedicated to Betsy:
Time wings silently by,
butterfly, cocoon me.

CONTENTS

PART THREE

PART ONE

CROCUS

You poke your head through the snow
to show your face, the first guest to arrive
before the hosts are ready. You ring the bell
dressed in your Easter outfit:
Violet Lady-killer, Ice Blue Pearl,
Star-veined Blue Bird.

You bring good news—a promise
nature will keep, a rumor
that will prove true. Yellow Saturnus,
White Snow-bunting. You scout ahead, fearless:
Jeanne d'Arc—fragile yet unflinching
in March's damp wind.

Maybe you long for the company
of your wild sisters, sirens who call
from your roots in the Mediterranean.
Or maybe it's enough to be here in New England
surrounded by your brave, colorful cousins—
the annual happy surprise,
the first harbinger of spring.

THE PRIVILEGED LIFE OF AN EFFETE CORPS OF IMPUDENT SWANS

Because Hummock Pond on Nantucket is a fly-by for swans
I found myself wandering out of the house periodically
to watch the flock float past the dock.
You may have watched them on lakes or ponds,

the way they fan out behind the lead swan
and silently part the waters,
preening all the while,
pulling their orange beaks in

to further elongate the elegant neck
and groom the perfectly white feathers;
startled into flight just off the water, they remain
close enough the keep their own reflection in sight

while winging their way across the pond.
They live not ascetically but aesthetically,
a life we can admire or try inadequately to imitate
in dance or art or perhaps even poetry.

But what would swans think of divorce,
abuse, drive-bys, road rage,
blood ballets on the screen.
Tsk, tsk, they'd say, ruffling their feathers,
floating blissfully by, not an enemy in sight.

LETTING THINGS GO

Seemingly unstoppable, weeds send out roots,
tubers, runners, rhizomes. You ignore them
because they are beneath
contempt. Then one day out back
near the end of summer, you realize mint,
comfrey and sage have overrun the garden.
Those knee-high plants are pigweed!
That spray of white flowers alongside the garage—
Queen Anne's Lace. You yank thistle while walking,
bend over to get knotweed.
Then you're down on your hands and knees
pulling up burdock, filling your fists
with oxalis, healall, black medic.
Dirt flies in your face and eyes.
When you catch the back of your wrist
on the rose bush, you rub your brow
and the dirt streaks with red-tinged sweat.
Still you cull the weeds for hours on end
until the bloody sweat runs down
your neck and arms and your hands—
slippery as fish. Your eyes blur
as you rise to your feet—dizzy
and queasy in the August heat.
Piles of weeds line the driveway.
The remaining lawn marred with bald patches,
thatch and crabgrass. Take a closer look—
nutsedge, henbit, shephard's purse.
Now the weeds have gotten under your skin.
Can't you see the fatal mistake
of letting things go so long?

WALK OUT

If one night you return home unhappy, walk out.
Walk out of your house, down the street,
into the darkness, to the far end of the field.

When the woods loom up before you,
stop there and gaze up into the sky.
Crane your neck so stars fill your vision.

Then step between the trees and walk on.
When it is too dark to see
and you are tired and far from home,

stand absolutely still.
Hear crickets, flies, bats, an owl.
When the owl hoots, answer his question.

IN THE COUNTRY

Owls find each other
in the dark
by calling. Here
the darkness falls
like a hammer
and I call your name—
the sound reaches
into the night
like a hand. And I feel
you out there
just beyond my grasp.

And there is an owl
I hear, up all night
like me, singing
his onerous song
out of instinct
and longing. I
watch him glide
over the moonlit grass
searching
for anything
that moves.

SOME TREES

Some trees seem to know it's cold.
Like old clothes, lost leaves
are left behind to rot and change
to the moist mulch of spring
when anything might take root and grow.
And I know I ought to throw old clothes away,
but can't quite bring myself to,
and so I find the worn collars of desire
hanging in the storage closet of my heart.
On such days memory is an overcoat,
frayed at the sleeves,
moth-eaten with regret.
Nonetheless, I don the coat
and go for a walk.

Is it you I see
out of the corner of my eye?
No, only a tree,
stark and quivering.

THE WAY WE LIVE

Driving to work on a cold November morning
I spotted out of the corner of my eye
a red-tailed hawk clutching a dead squirrel in his talons,
winging his way across Pleasant Street
to alight on the leafless branch of a birch.

I stopped the car and got out to look.
The crows were raising a racket.
In the suburbs they own all road-kill.
The hawk thought otherwise.
I told him: Take off! Head for the Blue Hills
where you can feast in peace.

He held his beak up and gazed down at me
with his superior vision. Then he pushed off,
stretched his wings and flew into the woods.
As I watched his red and white speckled tail feathers fade,
I remembered the motor running—I was late. I thought,
we have to change the way we live.

THE POET RAKES LEAVES

Everyone knows the falling leaves are a metaphor,
a synecdoche to be precise, because exactness
is important in poetry although it is by no means
everything. The leaves are a part of the whole fall.

The falling leaves stand for the fall
and the fall represents the autumn of life
which is of course followed by winter—
an allusion to King Lear? No,

that can't be right; it's the failure to think straight—
Lear's madness—that not only got him in trouble
but is a symptom of the autumn of life
when the leaves of memory flame to color one's days

before falling to the earth
to pile up in slippery, colorful clumps
we rake with the old bamboo rake
while the leaves tick past like seconds

to float down and pile up like old memories—
we rake to make sense of the past;
we think by looking—what is there to see
before the cold arrives like an old hag

rattling the bones of age. We rake
with the bamboo rake the brilliant red hands of maple,
elongated fingers of oak, yellow tongues of elm,

dried brown ears of chestnut, their spikey husks
clawed open by squirrels after the nut.
Isn't that what we're all after after all?

DIGGING TOO DEEP

On a cool moist morning in May
I dug too deep and found a seam—
a fetid odor rose like smoke.

The foul acrid musk set me back on my heels
and called to question my reason for being
out digging so early—

turning the earth over,
searching for rich worm-tunneled soil
to replenish the garden.

What I didn't need was this effluvium,
this putrid miasma of malodorous myrrh
emanating from somewhere down below—
some sulphurous cavern that runs deep

beneath the surface to the underworld
where a three-headed dog
takes orders from a scaly serpent
who speaks in tongues.

THE GARDEN

When the spring arrives you turn the earth over.
The long-handled spade brings worm tunnels to light.
Robins carry the feast to young beaks. You unearth
rocks, roots, colonies of ants. Heave

a stone the size of an elephant's foot
into the mulch pile behind the house,
catch sweat as it drips from your lip to your tongue,
break up clumps of dirt with a rake,

carve the furrows with the hoe; sow
the seeds which are the seeds of hope
because when you plant, you just might
get back what you put in.

So you persist, hose in hand—
the fine spray of water
from the reservoir in the hills,
more than you need.

What you want is another story.
What you want lies dormant
in the moist garden of your soul—
ever ready to sprout and grow.

THE OWL

The owl of sorrow sits on your shoulder.
You believe nothing you don't want to believe.
No matter what you do you grow older.

You've done your best to lie and deceive.
Everything you kept inside you told her.
The past is something you can't retrieve.

You feel the weight of time like a boulder.
Only a fool would believe what you believed.
The world goes on; it just gets colder.

Go ahead and ask. There's something you'll receive.
This life is cold and getting colder.
Sometimes it's all you can do to breathe.

SOMEONE IS CALLING

When the wind whips and whistles
past your ears, blows the hat
off your head, stands your hair
on end, and warps your sense
of hearing, so all you get are bits,
fragments of phrases,
clumps of words whose meaning
is lost, and try as you might
you can't quite put it together;
it doesn't make sense—
you're too far away.
You feel out of touch,
cut off, as if you are drifting
south on an ice floe—
melting as you go.
You reach back for shore.
You were that close moments ago.
Now it shrinks in the distance

and what's disappearing from sight
is home. Once we knew
how to listen in the wind,
which way to face,
how to put words together.
Now we shout from one precipice
to another and all we hear is an echo.

DROUGHT

What you do, you wait for a great drought to end.
Even if by then the stalks are gray
and the buds crumbling—day
by day, wheat so stiff
it breaks in your hand. And when
you look to the sky for rain,
you find no friend. Old friends
are best, they say. Then again,
the hungry stock need hay;
they're near the end. And the end
looms in the interminable haze
of unending noon and sun-drenched days.
So you wait—feet on parched land,
eyes on the sky, and an upturned hand.

GREAT BLUE HERON

The town had cleared the overgrown banks
of Pine Tree Brook,
leaving a swath
wide enough for walking.
I was on my way to Pope's Pond
where no-one ever seems to go
though the woods are littered
with empty cans of beer,
paper scraps and broken glass.
I was looking at my feet,
engrossed in thought.
I must have startled the heron
from his perch on the bank
overlooking the brook
in search of fish, frogs, mice
and birds naÔve enough to come too close.
He skipped directly across my path
on those crazy stick-like stilts,
yellow beak level with my chin.
He lifted his wings—wide as I am tall
and carried his airy body aloft
to the branch of a birch.
He was bigger than a swan
with none of the swan's elegant beauty.
He stared at the brook and squawked
like a crow with a cold. Ugly
and ungainly as he was,
it was grand to get so close
to a great blue heron
in the suburbs, and yet
it was strange,
crossing the line
between his world and mine.

14

CAUSE AND EFFECT

It isn't always what you expect.
You'd think the cacophony of birds disquieting.
Awake before dawn in their quest for food,
They chitter and chatter and cheep.
They whistle and chuck and cluck and squawk
as they search for seed, insects, worms and grubs.

Meanwhile, trails of trills hang in the air—
a-rhythmic fragments of song,
antiphonal notifications of arrival and departure,
telegrammed announcements,
invitations to family and friends,
warnings!

Don't they ever relax?
Their rites and rituals inhabit your waking dreams
and give pause to your day
with splashes of goldfinch yellow,
cardinal red and grackle blue,
rock dove pink and robin orange.

FIGHTING FIRE IN COLORADO

On good days, "You beat something back. You put
something down." But there are other days
when wind gets behind fire and whips it forward
up a hill faster than down,

feeding on crackling dry oak brush, pinyon and juniper.
The first of ten standard fire fighting orders
of the US Forest Service says, "Keep informed
of fire weather conditions and predictions."

But you can't always know which way
the wind will turn. Even trained smoke-jumpers,
helitackers, Forest Service hot shots,
third generation fire fighters...

On Saturday lightning struck a tree
igniting the brush. By Wednesday
100 acres were smoking black;
you spent the morning cutting a tree line

on the ridge between the fire and Glenwood Springs.
Mid-afternoon the wind picked up;
fire jumped the ravine, and burned up the slope so fast,
it sucked the oxygen out of the air.

The wind shifted and fresh air flash-fired the valley
until the entire canyon was engulfed.
You flailed away with axes, saws and hoes
while birds burst into flames.

16

You tried to run but the air was gone
so you climbed into an aluminum cocoon
hoping for change and you got your wish
when your lungs collapsed and gave flight to your soul.

AT THE BEACH ON THE HOTTEST DAY OF THE YEAR

On a Sunday afternoon in August
I'm stretched out floating like a jellyfish
in the ocean at Crane's.
Sky azure, white cumulus anchored on the horizon,
water warm as a cat's purr.
Waves rock me side to side.
Through my eyelids the sun burns.
Gulls and terns call fish to surface.
Disembodied voices and music dance on shore.

If I could move I might find the bottom with my feet,
wade back in and fall under the reign of the sun
so near its zenith this time of year
in the northeast of North America.
Instead I remain suspended, belly up,
eyes closed to time, which goes by, I guess, without me.
As if I'd left my body behind and become
nothing more or less than thought
buoyant as a bubble in the air.

CISCO BEACH, NANTUCKET, 1995

There were four houses there last year,
the cabbie said, pointing to the empty shore
when he dropped me off at the cottage.
One had been moved inland, the others
washed out to sea. The landscape was littered
with dead, twisted pines, some cut down to stumps.
High tide filled what was left of a foundation
at the edge of the dunes. The waves rolled
and roared ceaselessly—sometimes
they doubled up to arch in waterfalls
above my head. But I knew how to swim
in big waves, and dove that day
between the breaks to surface
and bob in rollers, and ride
the riptide to where I thought the waves
would throw me up onshore; instead
they flipped me under and dragged me along
until I surfaced, gasping and weary.

That night the two-room shack shook,
the wind whistled, the ocean growled
and I drowned in my dreams.

At dawn I woke unsteady and walked the plank
that lead from my door to the beach
where the undertow pulled the sand beneath my feet.
You'd think three-quarters of the earth's surface would be
enough.

JUST BEFORE SUNSET IN DECEMBER

It must have something to do with the angle of the earth
as it turns away from the sun in late fall in New England
when just after four the temperature drops
and the light shoots straight from the hip of the horizon
striking maples, elms, birches and oaks
whose leaves curl up on the ground, dry and lifeless,
while the sun flashes yellow through the trees
as if to say, slow down, look both ways.

This must be what the Impressionists were after
afternoons in Brittany when the tide was out
and the long flat sand pinned the light in crystals,
the water a host of concave mirrors—
buoyant with the promise of art.

While here and now this stark luminosity,
coolly transparent, is oddly uplifting
as it streaks red across the sky
and singes the clouds orange.

Yeats said, in balance with this life, this death.
Maybe that's why we are given this gift of light
or maybe we just see it that way
as a reason for pausing, however briefly,
grateful to be alive.

PART TWO

FIRST GRADE

The week before school begins he has nightmares:
Bugs as big as dogs crawl under the covers;
his friend Joey's eyes pop out and roll on the floor;
a hand grabs him by the neck and won't let go.

He cries out, "Mom! I'm scared. Can I come in your room?"
"OK," my wife says sleepily. I get up,
and he takes my place in the double bed
while I climb in between Softie and Blankie.
On the wall behind my head, the universe
illuminated by the nite-light.

Tomorrow he will take his seat
in Room 201 with twenty-nine other boys and girls.
The ferry of hope will carry him through the day
while just beneath the surface anxieties lurk like sharks.

He is ready to turn the key to numbers
and solve the mystery of money,
to open the book of reading
and grasp the power of the written word.

Yet he fears failure, which swirls beneath him
like a whirlpool. And he fears
the hand of change,
which comes and grabs him by the neck
just when he's getting comfy.

BUGS

"Dad come quick. Look—
a bug eatin another bug."
I'm out the door and across the street,
coffee cup in hand. They're at it again.
Seven am in August and the boys:
John, 5, Eddie, 6, Joe, 7, are hunting bugs.
The big plastic jug stuffed with grass and twigs—
air holes in the lid—sits on the steps.
Grasshoppers climb the twigs.
A cicada, wings crumpled, green eyes opaque in the sunlight,
floats on its back in the water at the bottom.
"Too much water!" Joe calls. "They're drowning."
Joe removes the cover to dump the water.
"No! No!" Eddie yells as grasshoppers leap to freedom.
A ladybug—orange shell, black dots—lands on my wrist.
"Good luck," John says smiling.
Eddie puts the cover back.
The praying mantis never seems to notice.
"It's a robber fly!" John yells pointing at the ground.
We crowd around and count five empty carcasses—
the remains of the robber fly's feast.
"It's a true fly," Joe says. Eddie nods
having killed his first housefly with a karate chop
the night before. He picked it up by a wing,
counted six legs and dropped it in the trash bucket
beside his bed. "Got it!" John says
snaring the robber fly in his net.
"Is a fly who kills other flies
good or bad?" I ask.
John shrugs, puts the fly in the jug
and snaps the lid shut.

LOOKING BOTH WAYS

In this photo circa 1988, you lean forward
at eight months, propping yourself up
on the edge of your blue plastic pool—
water down around your knees.
(I hold your arm to keep you from going under
  while your mother takes the picture.)
Your mouth turns up in a toothless smile.
Your brows arch above your eyes—
hopeful and expectant—your eyes smile too.
What is the source of your happiness?
The cool water of the pool?
The heat of the sun?
The warmth of our love?
Whatever it is, you appear to be ready
to climb out and spring into life
without guile, without doubt, without a moment's hesitation
as if you were born sure-footed
with the sun at your back, life
an open field on a June day full of green and promise.

I want to say, Yes.
No, for Christ's sake
be careful. Look both ways
before you leap; wear a hat;
write your name in your glove;
learn to do well, seek justice.
I want to hold on
to your arm—give you support,
but know I can't protect you
from harm, hatred, jealousy, scorn,

accidental drowning, tornadoes, lightning,
the undertow, drunk drivers,
overworked air-traffic controllers,
burnt out mechanics,
bus drivers on drugs,
terrorists.

God, Satan, Fates, angels, luck,
let me die first.

THE LIFE WE LEAD

Sometimes I wish that I could get away;
The distant song of angels stills the air;
I look at you I know I want to stay.

Walk out the door; the fields were made for play.
Look hard enough; it will all come clear.
Sometimes I wish that I could get away.

If I could just get through the grief I'd say
You cannot build your life around your fear.
I look at you I know I'd like to play.

This life we lead it makes us pay and pay.
We lose sight of everything we hold dear.
Sometimes I wish that I could get away.

You tell me you don't know just what to say.
Take the wheel and you will learn to steer.
Sometimes I wish that I could get away.
I look at you I know I want to stay.

PICKING UP THE KIDS PRAYER

Please God let me make this green light
so I won't be late and keep the kids waiting
in the playground where they could be abducted
by the known abuser who lives in the beautifully maintained
white Colonial with the black shutters just down the street.
Please God don't let me get stuck behind a blue-haired
octogenarian in a late-model Cadillac with Florida plates
or a mother against drunk driving,
(they always drive the speed limit)
and you know I haven't driven drunk, 80 miles per hour,
no lights
on side streets at 3 am for years—I've reformed.
I drink at home alone operating no heavy equipment
other than the remote. Please God let me make
the yellow light before it turns
because I have to get the kids home
and get back to work on my laptop
I'm already way behind and it's only Monday.
I promised their teachers I'd get the kids off
on the right foot this term,
doing their homework before watching TV,
after stickball and soccer and skateboarding,
because they need to know how to focus
and meet deadlines and never ever fall behind.

TURNED TO STONE AT THE REMBRANDT EXHIBIT

My six year old and I went to see plump, rosy-cheeked women—
bulbous beauties of another age. Instead
we found ourselves transfixed by Medusa's head
hanging from the hand of Perseus—
snakes for hair and hair everywhere,
globules of blood dripping
from where the neck had been.

We'd just read about Perseus the night before.
Call it coincidence or fate. Eddie sat on my shoulders—
both of us unwilling or unable to move.

That night he woke up crying and climbed into bed
with my wife and me. In our arms the snakes
turned back to hair. In our eyes he found the shield
that caught Medusa's dangerous stare.

SAVE THE DAYLIGHT

Twice a year we fiddle with time:
springing forward and falling back.
We manipulate the hands of the old clocks,
hit buttons on the new ones—
the only time in our lives we defy the sun
while the earth revolves beneath our feet.

Even now, as you read this, sitting or standing,
you too are in motion—moving away from birth,
toward death, through ages
which never feel quite right.

I am eight years old today! my son proclaimed
on waking this morning. And I have to remind myself
I'm still relatively young at forty-four
although I don't feel young.

And do you feel your age?
Or do you feel as young as ever—
a child in the body of a man,
a young girl in the clothes of an old woman?
Spring forward. Fall back.

ODYSSEUS

When I was young you were a hero to me—
you balanced wit and strength in harmony.
The army chose you over Ajax to lead the men.
Wise Odysseus they called you, more than friend.
You knew when to fight and when to refrain.
And I, if in trouble, invoked your name.
Cleverness over force, to myself, I'd say.
I'd fight if I had to—for friends, I'd stay.
Though the times I backed down, I'd wonder aloud,
Was there reason still to remain proud?
It was no surprise to me when you strung your bow,
your enemies sitting targets in a row.
Telemachus had their weapons under lock and key.
They'd taken advantage of your hospitality,
and tempted the faithful Penelope.
Now they would have to pay your fee.
And I was with you as the arrows flew
and found their marks; your aim was true.
The blood of Greek men stained the floor
and coursed in streams out the door.
Telemachus and Penelope must have cried,
Did so many have to die?
Surely they questioned who you were—
how you'd been altered after the war.
Today we wonder what it means.
Do heroes exist only in dreams?
Those of us who believed in you
without your wit, or your strength to see us through.

ANTIGONE

Others lied and deceived but you believed.
You'd lost one brother to another
and when he lay slain you chose between
the laws of the King and what you saw

as higher law. And for your pains
what did you receive? No personal gain—
death at the hands of Creon, the King.
While your betrothed—Creon's son,

so bereaved, having lost a wife
took his own life. Today,
you almost seem naive and yet
we pay homage to you, Antigone.
Others lied and deceived
but you believed what you believed.

MIRROR

Light-catcher
hole in the wall,
old, cold friend.
Duplicitous by nature,
never natural.
Mimic. Mime.
Wordless rhyme.
Tattletale.
Cool, cruel,
never the fool.
Not you. Not you.

You remain the same—
unfeeling while we change.
You expose every flaw:
weak chin, mealy mouth,
thinning hair, thin skin.
What you see may well be
true but sticks to the surface
like ice. You reflect
what others fail to see,
what we deny.
Unfairest of the fair,
I know you are
but what am I?
Mirror. Mirror.

PACHYSANDRA

Who could have foretold when seven years ago
we planted pachysandra on the east side of the house
to cover a strip of soil beside the driveway,
how she would flourish, ravenously devouring leaves,

chips of paint, tennis balls, bricks and coins.
But when we caught her choking the azaleas,
you cried, "Enough is enough!"

We bent from the waist and pulled her out in fistfuls,
until green clumps potted the driveway
and ugly white tubers stuck up like twisted antennae.
We dug in with shovels and turned the earth over.

Still the roots remained in an intricate web
that ran three feet deep. We fell to our knees
to knead the rocky clumps and yank the fibrous roots

till the dirt peppered our arms and blackened our faces.
"We won't get it all," I said,
smearing the brown-streaked sweat on my brow.
We stood back and surveyed the ravaged strip of earth.

It wasn't pretty. We were done
but not finished, finished but not done.
"Pack it in Cassandra," you joked.
We hesitated as if listening for an answer.

FISHING WITH MY DAUGHTER

Undulating waves break on jagged rocks.
Wooden boats knock against the docks while you cast
from the end of the pier. I cut and set the bait
and from my vantage point I peer
and get you in my sights.

It is your legs I see first—
the cable of muscle that runs
from your calves to your thighs.
You hook a bass and your legs flex.

You pull the rod against your hips
and the rod arcs like a bow.
I run up yelling, Give it slack!
But you've already let out the line
so the bass can run.

I hear you say, "Reel and Run. Reel and Run."
And I see there's nothing more
you have to learn from me—
nothing you don't know now.

PRAYER

If you hadn't named him you could say
it wasn't meant to be.
If you had another boy,
you could wipe the slate clean—
use the name again.
But you never had another boy...

John is your name too and sometimes
when someone calls, you hear an echo.
On weak days you listen and succumb to the sadness
which is a lake you fall into fully clothed
to emerge cold to the bone.

At such times you wonder who he might have been,
how he would have sounded when he laughed.
He spent less time out of the womb than in it.

Today you would know early on.
But back then they couldn't see inside the womb,
couldn't tell if a baby's spine would fail to meet his brain.

Now, no-one in the family mentions the baby.
So, each year you kneel, light a candle, say his name.

AT THE END

For Bill Rooney

He was so old his bones seemed to swim in his skin.
And when I took his hand to feel his pulse
I felt myself drawn in. It was as faint
as the steps of a child
padding across the floor in slippers,
and yet he was smiling.
I could almost hear a river
running beneath his breath.
The water clear and cold and deep.
He was ready and willing to wade on in.

IN THE CITY ON YOUR FATHER'S SHOULDERS

You are taller than you will ever be.
You look down on college kids,
merchants, businessmen and women,
drug addicts, pan handlers.

Runners jog beneath you.
Flat tops of cars reflect heat,
cluttered beds of pick-up trucks tumble by.

The sun makes you squint,
so you turn away from the rays,
to stare at whomever you please.

They look up to you
with hopeful, open faces
reserved only for children.
Complete strangers smile and say hello.

Sometimes you smile back,
single clap your hand.
For now, on your father's shoulders,
you are riding high, above the fray.

THE LANGUAGE OF THE LISTENING EYE

Gaugin called painting
the language of the listening eye
which is why you should always keep
your eyes open. That way
you won't get paint in them.

Painting while listening to Tool,
for example, can be overwhelming.
Listen: that's not what we're after
here at the academy.

We're after much more—
eyes that hear; ears
that see a way out
of this morass, a role
for art in our age,
poetry that matters,
that makes us see
the world, listening
like Gaugin with our eyes.

LET'S TALK

"Remember when we almost hit that cow?"
I crack up laughing when I think of it.
You'd think I would be used to it by now—
you tip the bottle up to take a hit.
"Tell me what to do; I'll try," you say
and stop me as I reach out for the door.
"Come on, let's talk," you pull me back to play.
My eyes glaze over waiting for the war.
You seize my wrists and dig your nails, "don't start."
Your tongue is forked you've told so many lies.
You trace the scar that runs beneath my heart.
I cup your breast while searching in your eyes.
"If I could kiss away the pain, I'd try."
"You'll never kiss away the pain," you sigh.

WHO WE LOVE

Who we love we love for who they are.
How we meet seems more by chance than fate.
Say you decide to walk and leave the car
Although it means you will in fact be late.
And when you wait in line you find her eye.
Perhaps she looks like someone you once knew.
You introduce yourself—give it a try.
Don't admit that you don't have a clue.
You have to hope that she will not say no.
You reach out as if grasping for a prize.
In time you'll learn more than you need to know.
Well isn't romance faith in disguise?
It isn't what we think but what we feel.
Sometimes it's best to get right down and kneel.

PART THREE

PHOTOGRAPH

It isn't really you.
It makes you look
fat, your face
broad, hips wider
than I remember.
It skims the surface
of reality, Holmes said.
And yet your eyes
seem to be
pools of sorrow
I could wade in,
or is wallow
a better word?
Some words are better
than others, as are lovers,
and children, mothers
and fathers. If only
doing your best was enough.
If only you got out
what you put in...
The photograph is flat
and yet you seem to be
leaning toward me,
lips parted, ready for a kiss.
But that was years ago,
and that's the way
you remain: an image—
mute and unchanging
still

YOUR VOICE

Flipping through an old anthology,
I find a photo of you,
crouching in straw-colored,
wind-blown beach grass.

Blue down vest over white sweater,
head hooded in blue wool scarf.
At your back, sand dune cliffs
and a lime green sky.

Must have been a cold day in May,
yet you're laughing.
And looking at you
20 years later,
I laugh too.

I can still hear
your voice—warm
and low as a foghorn
on a misty summer night.
Suddenly I remember,
it wasn't just fun
we had together.

DENNIS MARTIN

1.

Dennis Martin couldn't wipe the smile off his face
to save his life.
"You think this is funny?" the principal would ask,
fingering Dennis' chest. "Look at me,"
he'd say, backing him into a wall.
He was a big boy—six-two, 220, sophomore year.
A natural, coaches said, but he couldn't keep

the foolish grin off his freckled face.
Shaking their heads, they'd send him home.
Kicked off three teams by senior year,
One spring day he walked out of school,
And never came back.

2.

You don't need a diploma to clean the emergency room
of Boston City Hospital where he had access
to every pharmaceutical imaginable.
He needed every one to keep the smile on his face,
mopping up the night's bloody remains.

"Dead man's shift," he joked with me, last time I saw him.
By then he was a spindly scarecrow, pale and shaking—
an ill-wind ululating within.
The freckles on his face stood out like scabs.
A month later he OD'd.
At the wake the casket was closed.
I'd like to think they couldn't wipe the smile off his face.

MIKE BERNIER

Mike Bernier was a dead shot from the corner.
I'd feed him on a fast break
knowing he'd make it good.
Like me, he had an attitude.
Coach Kudo kept him after practice for drills.
My friend Richard caught Kudo one night
pummeling Mike in the showers.
Halfway through the season
Mike didn't show up for school.
Two weeks later the principal announced
on the crackling loud-speaker
Mike had died of a mysterious kidney ailment.

Mike's old man was a disciplinarian.
Richard said he'd told Kudo to keep the kid in line.
It could have been Kudo or his dad
who did Mike in—hitting him one time too many
where the bruises wouldn't show.
In those days we didn't question
A fourteen year old dying
of a mysterious kidney ailment
though we all wondered aloud about Kudo
who pushed us up against the lockers
for fooling around in Health
and lifted us by our hair
for failing to tuck in our shirts.

Louis Cook was the one who finally KO'd Kudo
one afternoon in the parking lot after school.
That Kudo never reported it should've told us something.

Me, he liked because I'd suckered a guard from Dedham
who got away with fouling me under the boards.
Take it easy, Tiger, Coach Kudo said to me on the bench,
his smile more of a sneer. We understood each other.
I smiled back.

THE WAY WE DIE

I remember kissing Nancy Huffam
the summer after seventh grade
behind Richard Lang's house.
The stars illuminated her freckles
and in each sleepy eye—a moon rose.

At school in the caf
my friends and I watched her cross
her legs across the room
as we ate our ice cream sandwiches.

In high school she went out with upperclassmen,
then, college guys. At a BC party I heard
she got drunk and passed out in a bedroom
where one of the guys took off all her clothes.
It was just a prank. Senior year she fell asleep

in the back of a van that crashed
head on into a truck. She must have thought,
It's a dream. Or maybe, she never woke up.
Or maybe she woke up dead.

WHITE LIE

A stepped leader—zig-
zagging segments
of negative electrical charge—
pulses down
from the center of a cloud.
A streamer of positive energy
rises from the earth
to meet it.
That return stroke—
current surging up
through a channel in the air—
we call lightning.

Meanwhile, light's slow cousin,
sound, trails lazily behind:
when the lightning heats
the surrounding air
five times hotter
than the surface of the sun,
the air expands and vibrates
like a kettle drum.

At such times our senses
lose their bearings.
Our ears are fooled
and our eyes lie.

THE QUARRY

In March your feet froze
when you dangled them down
into the ice-blue water.
From the ledge you could see
the rusted body
of the Police Chief's Dodge—
the one Gito stole
and ran,
rock on the pedal,
off the jump they called
Angel's Heaven.

The antenna pierced Gito
one year later
when he jumped
through the trees.
A thin stream of watery blood
floated to the surface—
he survived with one lung.
That year the town dumped oil in the quarries
to keep us kids away.
Still, today, in the green light of spring,
the Police Chief's Dodge
glimmers like an echo
in the shimmering water.
Or is it here
beneath the oily surface
of your mind where
the old, vengeful vehicle rests.

BLACK ICE

Black ice is never unexpected
early mornings in October
in Vancouver. Unless you're from
the lower forty-eight
in which case you might be caught
off guard, when late
for hockey practice,
roads empty, feet heavy,
still waking up, coffee cup
in hand, you feel the vehicle sway—
rear wheels sliding toward
your shoulder—the jeep
suddenly amphibious,
caught in crosswinds,
turning crabwise,
steering wheel a broken rudder,
brakes a pedal to a missing bass drum—
you beat against time,
your sense of direction—
who you hoped to become—
a compass needle fluttering in fear
where your momentum carries you
off road and over a cliff
into thin air.

WATER

At home we use a charcoal filter
to prevent rust and the odor
of sulfur. Not that it's ever
colorless, odorless or tasteless.

I remember it sweet
in the Northern Kingdom
of Vermont, carrying the scent
of heather and pine and slate,
replete with shadows
shading rainbow trout—
the river a chameleon of color,
repository of life and meeting place
of deer, beaver, and occasional moose
who, like us, must find it hard to fathom
why it sometimes fails to freeze at zero
or remains frozen so late in spring
and seemingly melts all at once
to race downhill, overrun banks
and infiltrate fields where,
spring afternoons, greenheaded ducks
float indifferently by.

Cup it two-handed;
Take a quick drink
before it runs
through your fingers—
elusive as time.

DONKEY

To walk sure-footed, clippity clop, quick
yet focused on the matter at hand
which is nothing more or less than the earth
beneath your feet—the trail you follow

knowing by heart each twist and turn,
each bump, dip, hole, run-off, where it is smooth
and where the rocks gather, and when to lean
into the hill until your head

is nearly touching the ground
and the dust makes you snort
yet you keep on up the slope

until it levels out and the trail narrows
overlooking the canyon hundreds of feet below.

It's all the same to you as you chew a clump of crabgrass
and paw the rock while we take photos.
You snort with impatience, eager to get going again,
to return from where you came
though it isn't the destination that matters.
All that matters is getting there.

WANDERING BEHAVIOR

— In the U.S. 32,000 are reported missing annually.

One day without warning they walk out,
past stop signs posted by loved ones,
through doors disguised by curtains.
They head south like migrating birds
following an inner compass, unwavering
across roads, fields, highways

until they become entangled in brush
or stuck in a brier patch
or frozen at a fence line in a field.
Sometimes they are found bloated,
floating face down in a creek or a stream or a pond.

They may be trying to find a safe place to hide.
They may want to remain unfound in the woods.
Wandering behavior is as old as dementia itself
and all Alzheimer's victims behave much like each other.

Old Eskimos walked out to freeze on the ice.
Old Aborigines suspended themselves in trees in the bush.
Alzheimer's victims walk south, toward the light.

IF YOU LIVE

1

If you live to be old enough your body turns against you,
becomes your enemy, seems determined to fail you,
and you become uncomfortable in your own skin; yet
you accept this because it is the natural order of all living beings.
But if your body is overtaken by disease when you are still young
you feel wronged—one of the chosen—and you think
you must have made a mistake
going home with someone you barely knew,
you failed to take precautions, failed to take care of yourself,
sinned against the Father, the Son and the Holy Ghost—
living an unnatural life, following your heart
which betrayed you like all those you once thought friends
who abandoned you as soon as they noticed the lesions,
the loss of hair, the weight you shed like old worn out clothes
until you lay in a bed—skeletal as a malnourished child
only a mother could love, and your mother loves you still,
sees you as you were, holds your hand and weeps
for what you are, who you might have been.

2

Sometimes you were sure you knew who it was—
the tall blond handsome one with the sallow complexion—
but then you thought, Maybe not.
Mark said, it didn't matter; it was fate. Mark said
he'd have sex with anyone. It had nothing to do with him.
He was keeping all the bad thoughts out.
He was remaining positive, staying strong

because attitude was everything.
Brian said so too and Brian looked buff.
No one suspected him. Anyway
it wasn't unusual not to know who it was;
lots of people never found out.

It was like being adopted by the devil
or abandoned by God.
It was like being adopted and abandoned.

ODE TO A COLD

1

The Relation You're Obliged to Harbor

Around Thanksgiving
unannounced yet expected
he rolls in
like a fog off the ocean
until you can't see
where you are, caught
in a wave of inertia
unable to think: it's sink
or swim, and you're going
down—water fills your nose,
your eyes. Your ears ring:
Is no one home?
And no one answers:
You're on your own.

2

The Legacy

One day you wake to the sound
of the door closing. You can see
clearly now: you are yourself
again. But in the mirror
you find he's left his bags
under your eyes.

57

THE OLD MAN IN THE MEN'S ROOM

You see him standing before the urinal,
head bowed in silence, waiting,
intent upon the moment,
eyes closed in a kind of prayer.

Not to the porcelain god
who hangs on the wall,
open to any and all offerings.
But to his own body
which fails to follow
a simple order from the brain.

The message, lost in translation.
The language of the body—
the pleasure of movement, grace
quick feet, sure hands, now
foreign and unfamiliar
as a face he can't place
from where he stands,
holding his penis in his hand
like a cracked egg.

DIVORCE

By the time you're fifty if you're in your right mind
you want a divorce from yourself.
You've already tried a trial separation—
a week in the Caribbean, a month in Maine,
a windjammer cruise. You come back and think
you can begin anew
only to find nothing's changed
and that makes it all the worse.
So you join a health club
or hire a personal trainer
to whip you into shape.
You buy natural supplements,
begin a new diet, drink
more water, less booze. Switch
from ice cream to frozen yogurt.
You get a haircut that really fits your face.
You take dance lessons, music lessons, you learn
a new language. At night you return home tired—
older not wiser. How about hormone therapy,
Prozac, plastic surgery?
Forget about it. It's time to file for divorce.
Move to a new city. Leave behind
that fat lazy fool who returns your hopeful gaze
in cruel mirrors every morning
as you brush your caffeine-stained teeth.
He can have the house that needs painting,
the car that needs brakes,
the lousy art in the living room,
the oversized TV in the den.

This is the year to take a train into tomorrow,
one-way ticket in hand,
destination: somewhere new
where no-one knows your name
and you can be someone else.

SCHOOL SHOOTER

One sits silent and alone
in the chamber of the semi-automatic.
A brass jacket keeps his powder dry.

I eject him to check the action,
then put him back into the clip
above his nine other brothers—
perfect clones, my leaden friends.

They will all do as I say
when I exercise my will
over my index finger
to set them off like rockets.

I'll recoil from the echoing shouts
while my astronauts
wend their way home.

Don't blame the messengers
that fly from my hand
and announce my intentions,
sealing the secret pact I've made
with the enemies of my state.

AT WIT'S END

This is the street where horns blare and fenders crumple,
where grills are crushed and radiators hiss.
This is the cafÈ where lovers go toe to toe,
eye to bloodshot eye, fingers to chest,
hand to cheek, fist to face.

Welcome to wit's end where
hands tear hair out and curses fly.
This is the room where shirts are ripped,
noses broken, toes dislocated,
doors unhinged, windows shattered.
This is the bar where the fifth is drained,
where the gun is loaded and the safety's off.

This is the place where enough is enough;
the line is drawn. And you cross it unthinking,
driven beyond reason
by adrenaline-charged energy
into the realm of pure emotion.

FISHING IN THE FALL

The lake, gray as fate
on a bad day,
plain as my face
after 40 years. My mistake,
taking the boat out
so late in the fall
to fish for the rainbow trout
I've nearly caught
half dozen times.
I've felt him nibble and bite
and take the line
and eat my bait
and still elude the hook.
Now I look for signs
of life but the rain
conflates the lake and sky
while morning mist
obscures the shore.
I must be halfway out—
it's hard to tell from where I sit.
And if I stood to peer
above the mist, I'd risk
a fall—the loss of all my gear.
I'll just sit tight,
wait right here,
hope the sky will clear.

RUNNING

When you run you learn to listen
to your body: the tiny bones
of your feet as your shoes
tap the pavement—from sidewalk
to street and pad along
on tree-lined paths
accompanied by birdsong.

You grow to expect your quads
to respond, your calves
to urge you on, your wind
to answer the call
as you pass your mile markers.

On moist days your knees
creak, cranky beneath
thin skin, scar tissue,
tendons that strain
under your weight.

Only when you stop
can you hear your heart,
blood pulsing in
your neck, wrist, chest,
repeating this is what
we were meant to do.

YOYO

With you, walking the dog
is a walk in the park.
I let you out and reel you in.
I throw you down; you climb back up
or sleep at the end of the line—
spinning suspended—
going nowhere fast.

I snap you back
to the triangle of the cat's cradle.
Then drop you out and send you round
the world and back home
in a loop de loop.

You are a toy that defies
Newton's laws and flirts
with infinity. You keep
your secrets tightly wound
and hide in a pocket like a hand.

STILL LIFE IN THE DESERT

Sleep is the state stone loves best
in the cool shadows
of a moon-illumined night.
Wind worn smooth
in the dreamless desert
beneath a purple sky
where bold distant stars
exist eternally
in the past—
way back when
the stones were joined together
in breathless unison.
Now alienated
but not unhappy,
they sit unmoving
still.

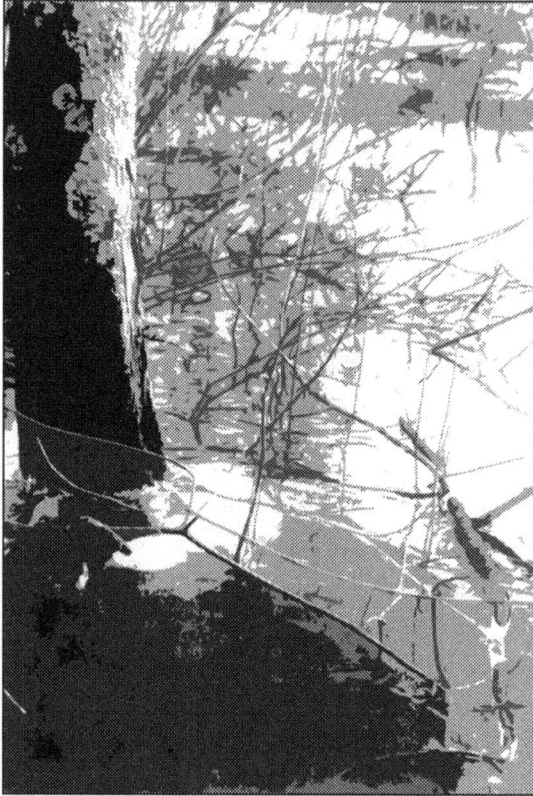

Printed in the United States

www.ingramcontent.com/pod-product-compliance
Lightning Source LLC
Chambersburg PA
CBHW032028090426
42741CB00006B/774